the zen of
snowy trails

the zen of
snowy trails

wit, wisdom, and inspiration

foreword by Kris Freeman
edited by Katharine Wroth
illustrations by Kate Quinby

SKIPSTONE

Kathleen Stocking quote excerpted from *Lake Country* (University of Michigan Press 1994). Kimberly Quinn Smith quote excerpted from *A Full Moon Rising ... and the Tao of Menopause* (Lulu.com, 2007). Tim Jones quote courtesy of www.easternslopes.com. Jeff Kildahl quote excerpted from *"The Holistic Snowshoer: Meditation," Snowshoe Magazine,* 2005. Sarah Ockler quote courtesy of http://sarahockler.com. Phil Dynan quote excerpted from *Brother Eagle, Sister Moon* (Self-published 2006). Florence Page Jaques quote excerpted from *Snowshoe Country* (University of Minnesota Press 1999). Jerry Apps quote excerpted from *Living a Country Year* (MBI Publishing 2007).

Published by Skipstone, an imprint of The Mountaineers Books
Manufactured in the United States of America

First printing 2009
12 11 10 09   5 4 3 2 1

Compiled and edited by Katharine Wroth
Illustrations by Kate Quinby
Design by Heidi Smets
Cover photograph © 2009 Monner/Dreamstime.com

ISBN 978-1-59485-273-2

Library of Congress Cataloging-in-Publication Data
The zen of snowy trails : wit, wisdom, and inspiration / foreword by
Kris Freeman ; edited by Katharine Wroth ; illustrations by Kate Quinby.
    p. cm.
  ISBN-13: 978-1-59485-273-2
  1. Winter sports—Quotations, maxims, etc.   I. Wroth, Katharine. II. Quinby, Kate, ill.
GV841.Z46 2009

  796.9—dc22

                    2009015070

Skipstone books may be purchased for corporate, educational, or other promotional sales. For special discounts and information, contact our Sales Department at 800-553-4453 or mbooks@mountaineersbooks.org.

Skipstone
1001 SW Klickitat Way, Suite 201
Seattle, Washington 98134
206.223.6303
www.skipstonepress.org
www.mountaineersbooks.org

SUSTAINABLE FORESTRY INITIATIVE
Label applies to the text stock

Certified Fiber Sourcing
www.sfiprogram.org

LIVE LIFE. MAKE RIPPLES.

Until you stand stock-still in winter woods, you don't really know the sounds of silence.

—Jules Older

world without end

by Kris Freeman

As a child, I spent hours at a time, whole days even, in a Superman cape. I believed that if I ran through the woods in my cape, I could take flight. I darted through the forest dodging branches, skipping streams, and jumping rocks and stumps in an imagined reality without limits. My abilities were thrilling, while the mental escape felt serene. As I grew older, I lost that imaginary world—but I no longer needed it. Skiing had filled the void.

My skiing education began even before the superhero fixation. My father instilled in me a love of snow sports when I was a baby, pulling me behind him in a sled as he strode down the parallel tracks of our local ski area. As soon as I could stand, he propped me up on skis, and I sensed the liberty of glide through my own feet for the first time. From that moment forward, all I wanted to do was take off over the snow.

I participated in my first cross-country race at the age of five. I finished in fifth place and was extraordinarily proud of myself. After the awards ceremony, my older brother informed me that there were only five racers in my class and that I had actually finished last. I was devastated, but instantly motivated as well. Two years later I won the same race. That was the beginning of the path that has led me to compete in two Olympics and five world championships, and to win an even dozen U.S. National titles.

There are all sorts of ways to find release in winter. Some people like the controlled steps of snowshoeing. Some like to set up camp and battle the elements. Some like just to breathe deep and take in the quiet of their surroundings. For me the best way is to take advantage of the physics of snow. Snow transforms the world into a giant playground where the regular rules of friction don't seem to apply.

What sets cross-country skiing apart from other skiing disciplines is that you never have to stop. Downhill skiing was actually my favorite for a time, but I tired of being interrupted by lifts and the long lines that accompany them. The rush of ski jumping had me hooked through high school, but the feeling—that exhilarating four seconds of hang time—was too short lived. In cross-country, I found abandon. I had to stop only when I'd gone as long and as far as my body would let me.

The more time I spent skiing, the stronger I became, and the more efficient my technique. The satisfaction I found in the sport swelled exponentially with this progression. Like a young hawk learning to predict and ride the wind's currents, I could cover more ground with less effort. I could dash through splendid forests and traverse to remote mountaintops with the ease of a soaring bird.

Skiing is not effortless even now, but the exertion becomes ever more sustainable and rewarding. The distance, duration, and speed of my skis know no limits but what I place on them. On a good stretch, I can make reality melt away—and find the same peace wearing skis that I once found while wearing my Superman cape.

let it snow

There's nothing like the sight of that first, fat, dancing flake to make the heart skip a beat. Winter is here, and a whole new season of splendors awaits.

The Great Snow! How cheerful it is to hear of!

—Henry David Thoreau

The snow had begun in the gloaming,
And busily all the night
Had been heaping field and highway
With a silence deep and white.

—James Russell Lowell

I ran today with a coworker, around noon, and suddenly we noticed it was snowing. As in: The First Snow of the Season. Big, fluffy flakes that took us completely by surprise. It made my day, and I raised my fists in triumph. Conversation froze, for a moment, as I smiled and watched the flurries flutter down. I breathed in deep, and the air seemed especially clean somehow. All was right with the world.

—Mark Remy

Snow provokes responses that reach right back to childhood.

—Andy Goldsworthy

It's a family joke that when I was a tiny child I turned from the window out of which I was watching a snowstorm, and hopefully asked, 'Momma, do we believe in winter?'

—Philip Roth

The first article I ever published, on a small printing press given to me on a snowy Christmas when I was six or seven, consisted of what was meant to be a report on snow depth in inches, and was distributed to neighbors. It read, in its entirety: "The snow 15."

—Cullen Murphy

There's always something magical about the first snow of the season—something that makes me nostalgic for winters passed. Something that makes me long for pink cheeks and sledding and hot chocolate with little marshmallows. Something that makes it okay to go outside on the front porch in the middle of the night with my husband in fuzzy pink snowflake and blue polar bear pajama pants (mine, his, respectively) to take pictures.

—Sarah Ockler

I picked up snow in my hand. I was amazed by how fluffy and feathery it was. I could see the individual crystals, and how they varied—I didn't know then that they were all different, of course. But the other thing that struck me was just how quiet everything was. I lived in the centre of this village and it was normally a noisy, busy place, but the snow deadened the sound. There was snow on every tree, every pavement, covering all the roads and so on. It had become a quiet world.

—Adam Watson,
79-year-old snow researcher on his first memory of snow

How the children shouted when the first white flakes came down! They caught them on their coat sleeves, and tried to find tiny stars.

—Etta McDonald

No two moments are any more alike than two snowflakes. Like snowflakes, they get that same look from being so plentiful and falling so close together. But examine them closely and see the multiple differences between them. Each moment has its own task and capacity, and doesn't melt down like snow and form again. It keeps its character forever.

—Zora Neale Hurston

Whenever a snowflake leaves the sky,
It turns and turns to say "Good-by!
Good-by, dear clouds, so cool and gray!"
Then lightly travels on its way.

—Mary Mapes Dodge

"I suppose it's naive to call snow magical," I whispered, entranced.

"Not if you think it is," Oscar granted.

—Sheridan Hay

I love snow, and all the forms
Of the radiant frost;
I love waves, and winds and storms,
Everything almost
Which is Nature's, and may be
Untainted by man's misery.

—Percy Bysshe Shelley

What I love about snow is that the one constant is its variability. What you see today isn't going to be out there tomorrow.

—Jill Fredston

Announce by all the trumpets of the sky,
Arrives the snow, and, driving o'er the fields,
Seems nowhere to alight: the whited air
Hides hills and woods, the river, and the heaven,
And veils farm-house at the garden's end.

—Ralph Waldo Emerson

The older I get, the greater power I seem to have to help the world; I am like a snowball—the further I am rolled the more I gain.

—Susan B. Anthony

The first fall of snow is not only an event, it is a magical event. You go to bed in one kind of a world and wake up in another quite different, and if this is not enchantment then where is it to be found?

—John B. Priestly

The snow itself is lonely or, if you prefer, self-sufficient. There is no other time when the whole world seems composed of one thing and one thing only.

—Joseph Wood Krutch

Getting an inch of snow is like winning 10 cents in the lottery.

—Bill Watterson

The first flake or flakelet that reached me was a mere white speck that came idly circling and eddying to the ground. I could not see it after it alighted. It might have been a scale from the feather of some passing bird, or a larger mote in the air that the stillness was allowing to settle. Yet it was the altogether inaudible and infinitesimal trumpeter that announced the coming storm, the grain of sand that heralded the ocean.

—John Burroughs

Snow sparkles like eyesight falling to earth,
Like seeing fallen brightly away.

—Wallace Stevens

Nature has no mercy at all. Nature says, "I'm going to
snow. If you have on a bikini and no snowshoes, that's
tough. I am going to snow anyway."

—Maya Angelou

The trail was white, the parking lot was empty and the day lay before us.

—Ron Dungan

on the move: walking, hiking, and tracking

Venture onto a snowy trail, and you're likely to notice two things: a scarcity of humans, and an abundance of evidence of non-humans. The rest is yours to discover.

The pleasures of winter are at once tricky to convey to the uninitiated and self-explanatory to the participant. The joys of winter hiking and camping are spectacular, subtle, and sometimes elusive.

—Michael Lanza

We put on our snow boots and lace them up so they are snug and comfortable. They feel warm. Our feet feeling warm makes our whole body feel warm. We walk outside and head out for a walk in the woods. Our feet landing in the freshly fallen snow feels new. Everything around us feels new. New, yet seasoned and wise.

—Kimberly Quinn Smith

The snow is so new and fresh that a microbe could walk across its surface and leave physical evidence of its passing.

—John Fielder

We shall walk in velvet shoes:
Wherever we go
Silence will fall like dews
On white silence below.
We shall walk in the snow.

—Elinor Wylie

I shall have a walk or two in my old haunts, among them beautiful woods. The snow will be out by that time; and, to my mind, there's no season when the woods look so well, and the air feels so fresh and free, as in a wintry day, with the ground all white, and wreaths of snow upon every vine and briar, and them great big hemlocks and pines rising up like black giants all around one. Some folks don't like the winter in the woods; but I could walk on, or go on, in a sleigh through them for ever.

—George Payne R. James

To travel in the moonlit silences, with tingling air and grotesque snow-covered pines and spruces looking like gargantuan specters, is really to live.

—Ellsworth Jaeger

A fresh blanket of snow that stops falling in the sunset hours gives an entire night's history of nocturnal animal activity the following morning.

—*Chicago Wilderness* magazine

Fluffy, ephemeral, matchless in its precision, and endless in its detail, the snow page displays the ways and whims of the great and small, of the thrifty and of the careless, of the roving hunters, of the home-abiding rodents; in fact, acting the part of a good newspaper, with partiality for the runners and walkers, while on rare occasions taking a short paragraph from the higher realms of the sky-fliers, quite like newspapers which men make of wood-pulp, plastered with ink …

—Raymond S. Spears

On the snow, as on a new white page, each animal prints its own indisputable narrative. Its footprints tell where and whence and how it ran. The leavings from its luncheon tell what and where and how it ate. The chips from its woodworkings, the scales from its huskings, or the earth from its diggings, tell how and where and why it labored. And if, by mischance, it fell a prey to some fierce foe, its blood-stained fur or feathers by the wayside tell how its little life ended in a tragedy.

—James George Needham

Travelers in snowfilled woods should not, by the way, expect to see a wealth of wildlife. Much of the time one moves through a white silence devoid of visible bird and animal life. Often one encounters nothing more than animal tracks and the chickadees, although sometimes one will be rewarded by a ruffed grouse bursting from a conifer, or, a rare delight, the same bird exploding from its sanctuary beneath snow that fell the night before.

—Nelson Bryant

The stillness and tranquility of the winter landscape is seldom spoiled by hordes of fellow travelers, and the winter traveler is not restricted to staying on trails, if, indeed, trails can be found at all.

—Kristi Anderson

In summer you round a corner expecting to see other hikers. In winter you round a corner and might see a branch swing after the rapid departure of a creature, or some other fascinating sign of solitude.

—Greg Johnston

Winter hiking is one of life's little-known pleasures.

—Jim Chase

I love the deep silence of the midwinter woods. It is a stillness you can rest your whole weight against … This stillness is so profound you are *sure* it will hold and last.

—Florence Page Jaques

Winter camping … is a way to experience the Earth during its darkest season—to discover a new world both physically and mentally.

—Victoria and Frank Logue

Resting on your laurels is as dangerous as resting when you are walking in the snow. You doze off and die in your sleep.

—Ludwig Wittgenstein

The snows of the winter woods and fields often reveal the comedies and tragedies in the daily lives of the woodfolk. Their life histories from day to day are faithfully inscribed in this vast blank page of the wildwood diary.

—Ellsworth Jaeger

It is the great challenge of the year, and we are all better for being tested by it. When else can a walk down a country road become a wrestling match with the elements, and when else does the icy air in the lungs speak so clearly of the delight of merely taking a breath.

—John Cole

Perhaps of all our untamed quadrupeds, the fox has obtained the widest and most familiar reputation …. His recent tracks still give variety to a winter's walk. I tread in the steps of the fox that has gone before me by some hours, or which perhaps I have started, with such a tip-toe of expectation as if I were on the trail of the Spirit itself which resides in the wood, and expected soon to catch it in its lair.

—Henry David Thoreau

The mice tracks are very pretty, and look like a sort of fantastic stitching on the coverlid of the snow. One is curious to know what brings these tiny creatures from their retreats; they do not seem to be in quest of food, but rather to be traveling about for pleasure or sociability, though always going post-haste, and linking stump with stump and tree with tree by fine, hurried strides.

—John Burroughs

Hard showers had swept over the mountains, wetting down the snow, keeping all the animals "close." Rabbits, squirrels, foxes, weasels, and all the other creatures were compelled to remain inactive. Then came the freeze of zero weather, bright sunshine, and the crust. We men felt the exuberance of the release from inactivity—so did other animals. The weasel's track showed how it rejoiced in the release.

—Raymond S. Spears

One day the temperature rises to thirty or more and I go for a walk. Snow falls. Soft as clouds, soft as cloud horses. I move through them as if I am riding a cloud horse, or as if I am a cloud horse, finding the road by the snow banks. Any day now a hot chinook, a fierce and maverick forty-mile-an-hour wind, will take down six feet of snow in three days, but for now I am in a dreamscape, meditating, merging with snow, feeling how it feels to submit to another reality.

—Kathleen Stocking

on the web: snowshoeing

Like traveling off the beaten path? You'll love snowshoes—and the fact that there's virtually no learning curve doesn't hurt. Just strap them on and go!

There is no better way to begin snowshoeing than just going and doing it.

—Snowshoe Magazine

A number of years ago, someone asked me why I didn't write a book on snowshoes and snowshoeing technique. I told them I could, but it would be the world's shortest book: "Attach snowshoes to feet, place one foot in front of other until destination is reached."

—Tim Jones

At first you need to keep your mind concentrated upon what your feet are doing; if you let it wander to the scenery, the results may prove disastrous. But once the stride has become instinctive, you hardly have to think about your webbed feet at all.

--Elon Jessup

If you can get around with swim fins on, you're already a snowshoe connoisseur.

—Marc J. Soares

It feels like you have wings on your feet.

—Gail Garman

I'm glad I did not fall on my face.

—Gymnast Nadia Comaneci, after trying snowshoe racing

I love to stride through a meadow that looks as if it's dotted with tiny trees, knowing that the 3-foot-tall evergreens are actually the tips of 30-foot firs. I revel in the freedom to wander where I please, aware that the deep snow protects the fragile alpine ecosystem from my footfalls and tent.

—Dan A. Nelson

Why do snowshoers snowshoe? Why? Well, because we can! Because we're good at it! And because we desire to become a better person because of it! Being fit makes us more capable individuals. Being outside makes us tough and teaches us to respect nature. Going to the wild white yonder where all is quiet except the sound of our breathing and the crunch of the snow makes us more at peace and calms and clears our mind for the real world.

—Danielle "Nellie" Ballengee

The snowshoer can pass up the groomed trails, open woods and meadows favored by skiers and penetrate the gloom of a hemlock swamp, a tangle of bushes and blowdowns, or the snarl of treetops and branches left by loggers.

—Nelson Bryant

When you're snowshoeing, it's a magic carpet that will carry you wherever you wish, if you are patient and take your time.

—Bob Frisch

Snowshoeing is to winter sports what solar energy
may someday be to the fuel crisis. You can't be charged
for walking.

—Rinker Buck

There are no defined parameters, no graded pistes, no times to beat—just you and the snow and wherever you want to go.

—Hilary Sharp

We lace up our snowshoes and bang them hard against the crust. A rust color is on the bark, and the sun is making purple shadows behind the trees. From time to time the light sends up a sheen of pocked glass ... The stillness of the forest is always a surprise, as if an audience had quieted for a performance.

—Anita Shreve

Snowshoeing is so silent that you'll hear snow tumbling from pine boughs, the wavering whine of the wind, and the crack of trees in cold, clean air.

—Dave Getchell

I walk like a duck when snowshoeing, my feet farther apart than normal so the snowshoes don't clank together. I stop often and look back at my tracks, for as difficult as snowshoeing may be in fresh, deep snow, the tracks are something to behold. They look like the tracks of some prehistoric animal that has visited the land once again and chose winter to do it.

—Jerry Apps

Part of the reason we engage in snowshoeing is its purity. Winter imparts its own pureness to accentuate the clarity and heighten the awareness of the moment. An inner-directed snowshoer will become part of this experience versus merely "doing" it. There is much more to snowshoeing than slogging about in the snow.

—Jeff Kildahl

I have gone miles and miles on snow-shoes when there was no other path than the glorious and perfect one made by the freshly fallen snow, and even though the landmarks were changed, the general courses were easily determined, and the joy of snow-shoeing is that one can go over ravines (a hundred, two hundred feet deep in snow), over precipices, over chaparral, over bad-lands, over rivers, creeks and the ordinary obstructions that compel deviations from a straight course during *good* weather, and pay little or no attention to them. There is a freedom, a delight, an exhilaration in thus riding or walking—no, gliding—straight ahead, on the snowy surface, over places where one must cautiously and laboriously climb in summer weather, that words fail to express.

—George Wharton James

To be a snowshoer is to be part of a curious and unique breed. We're a mix of wanderlust and foolhardiness—the wild and artful peace-seekers of the world.

—Marc J. Soares

For once, what makes a sport so appealing to people is the raw, unmediated experience of the thing—it's the woods themselves, and the mountains, and the entranced hush of moving through a country muted by snow.

—Peter Heller

The myriad stars sparkled with a cold brilliancy in that deep northern sky. The cypress-covered hills looked black as ebony against the fair white covering which stretched o'er lake and barren shore. No sound, save the creak, creak of our snowshoes, came to break the solemn wonder of that silence. The wind in gentle gusts blew the powdery snow against our cheeks, which were beginning to glow with the stirring exercise of tramping.

—F. Houghton

[A]bove the crunching of the snowshoes you can hear and feel the night. Maybe it's a snowy owl or the far-off bark of a coyote, but the night is alive and shrouded in a bluish haze. It is the stuff of horror movies, but it is also mesmerizing and a full-blown Zen experience.

—Kim Kinrade

Ordinarily, I prefer backcountry scenes that are free of evidence of man's passing, even if I'm one of the men in question. The exceptions are ski and snowshoe tracks, both of which I consider beautiful. I can live with ski and snowshoe tracks at least partially because they are so ephemeral. When the next storm blows in, they'll be covered or swept away. Ski and snowshoe tracks, in this regard, are performance art. And the foundation of that performance is built upon joy and rapture.

—John Fielder

on the edge: cross-country skiing

Those with a need for speed choose skis as their mode of transport—but backcountry gliding and climbing still offer plenty of time for rumination.

Cross-country skiing is great if you live in a small country.

—Steven Wright

At one time, being adventurous meant changing your granola mix and committing a spree of fashion crimes in solitude. No wonder some Nordic skiers have a reputation for being reclusive, pedantic, mulish and a bit odd.

—David McMahon and Lise Meloche

There is something very spiritual about cross-country skiing. It really moves me. Sometimes I see it as an art form.

—Bill Koch

There is something extraordinary about the motions of cross country skiing, the way one can get lost in it gliding down the track, hypnotically floating in this strange, white world. It's a bit like dreams of flying, floating down the track blessed with a grace you don't deserve, part of a beauty you've only observed from the outside. It's a way to get lost, to forget oneself, to feel strangely, wonderfully, different.

—Stuart Stevens

I believe that it is the mosaic of landscape, companionship and wildlife that strum the strings of my soul on skis.

— Jim Dale Vickery

You must feel the tug of your muscles as you near the top of a long grade, and know the joy of making your own track down an unbroken expanse of powder snow. … This is skiing. This is adventure!

—Jackrabbit Johannsen

I like to ski cross-country, which just means I'm in it for the long haul. I like to take off on my own. It is as fast or slow as you want it to be. Gives a person the chance to think.

—Phil Dynan

While the physiological benefits are clear, there is also a spiritual benefit. It's very helpful in clearing your head. I do some of my best thinking out in the woods.

—Charlie Yerrick

[C]ross-country skiing constitutes my most constant, enduring winter activity. I'm stronger, happier, and almost certainly saner because of it. Skiing has given me what backcountry guide Allan Bard called "a quiet mind and a satisfied soul."

—Jules Older

Even in a country like my Norway, where skiing has been utilitarian transportation for centuries, countless thousands, young and old, take to the hills and meadows every weekend for the sheer joy of skiing.

—Kaare Rodahl

Ski uphill? Or on level ground? Sure thing. Ski in the city park or the north woods without lessons or broken bones. Start at any age, with no costly investment in equipment. Ski free of noise, resort traffic, and those endless queue-ups for lifts. In short, ski cross-country.

—Charles E. Maurer

Cross-country skiing offers the most adventure for the least time and effort of any other sport. All you need is a snow-covered hill close to home. Put your skis on and zigzag to the top. Have lunch. Relax. Rest a spell. Then ski back down. There you have it—just possibly the first ascent and descent on skis of that particular piece of earth.

—Steve Hindman

For me, cross-country skiing isn't just a means of exercise. It's a way to reconnect with the natural world through a lovely rhythm that celebrates gentle movement, a calm mind, and a soulful sense of being one with the outdoors.

—Angie Cannon

Unburdened by heavy equipment and with no need to be confined to lift systems, helicopters or prepared pistes, you are free to explore remoter and wilder terrain. To pull off the prepared track at will and weave your way through the forest, down through fresh, deep snow, the scattered tracks of birds and rabbits the only sign that life abounds even in such apparently barren winter landscapes …. Alpine skiing may provide more thrills and spills, but for me, the real excitement of winter lies in this discovery of inaccessible places.

—Jen Harvey

You're striding along mindlessly and it suddenly hits you—the frost on the trees, the clouds of your own breath, the rays of sunlight splashing down through the branches, the intense quiet. The skiing becomes easy, effortless and serene. At that instant, the cosmic factors of snow, temperature, sunlight, motion and funky Nordic karma converge, and skiing becomes a kind of wintry Zen experience.

—Dave Buchanan

It's peaceful and doable.

—Cross-country ski student

It is a peaceful workout that completely taxes one's body.

—Nat Ross

The kick-glide, kick-glide rhythm dominated my senses almost to the exclusion of all else, and for a few brief moments, I thought I could ski forever. Then, of course, I lost the rhythm and the magic moment evaporated. But from then on I knew what I was looking for and found it more and more frequently, until wobbles and missteps were increasingly rare exceptions to a process that became so natural that I could leave my body on autopilot while my mind ran its own course, relaxed and free.

—Rick Lovett

There's something magical about gliding on the snow through the trees. It's a feeling that's almost like doing yoga on skis.

—Colleen Cannon

It is a silent stream swirling around boulders piled high with marshmallow puffs of snow, water gurgling under intricately designed ice. It is ripping turns through untracked powder, friends laughing as they glide through gently falling snow. It is going fast, pushing your body to its limit, or sliding slowly, quietly along at a pace of your own choosing—from breathing hard to hardly breathing.

—Barbara Corbett

I glide to a stop and gaze at the islands of snow in the river. A bird chirps. The water whispers. I breathe deep, my mind approaching wintertime Zen.

—Eric Peterson

You're out there and it's so quiet. It's just your breath, your heartbeat and you … You're surrounded by a thousand points of light from every snowflake or tree branch that's angled to catch the moonlight. All of that is why night skiing appeals to me.

—Mike Sayre

I know in my heart that it is a very strong sport that will always be with us. I certainly plan to ski all the days of the rest of my life.

—Bill Koch

winter: the last words

Just as the first snow brings joy to lovers of winter sport, the first signs of spring bring some sadness. Luckily, there's always next year—and winter's lessons always stick.

We don't just look forward to the first snowfall, we seek it. And spring brings mixed emotions, even sadness, as we watch the last snow disappear.

—Chad McGrath

I walked abroad in a snowy day;
I asked the soft snow with me to play;
She played and she melted in all her prime,
And the winter called it a dreadful crime.

—William Blake

What has been hidden by snow is revealed by a thaw.

—Swedish proverb

Without having experienced the cold of winter, one cannot appreciate the warmth of spring.

—Chinese proverb

The stars no longer gleamed with the cold glitter of points of brittle ice; in their gleam was a certain tinge of softness, as if the Winter crispness in them had thawed. The clouds that drove northward were not Winter clouds. Snow they contained, perhaps, but … their textures betrayed the fact that Winter had lost its stern grip on the heavens. The break-up was on its way.

—Henry Oyen

Many joys hath Winter brought
Underneath his rugged coat;
When at length his race is run,
Many joys with him are flown;
Flowers are sleeping 'neath his snows,
Bless old Winter ere he goes!

—S.F.C. (The Religious Magazine and Monthly Review)

You can't get too much winter in the winter.

—Robert Frost

Because it requires liveliness, winter makes all of us feel most alive, and knowing the sense and wonder of being alive is a true and important wisdom.

—John Cole

If wilderness is a tonic for a city-weary soul, a fine day in winter is a double shot.

—Greg Johnston

Winter is the main fact of our year, and the deepest mystery.

—John Elder